Kindle Paperwhite User Guide:

The Best Paperwhite Manual to Master Your Device

Get the MOST of what the Kindle Paperwhite has to offer

By Sharon Hurley

I0011332

Also check out Sharon Hurley's User Guide for the Kindle Fire!

Kindle Fire Manual: The Original Kindle Fire User Guide

http://www.amazon.com/Kindle-Fire-Manual-Original-ebook/dp/B00AMNK5OQ/

Table of Contents

Introduction

The Kindle Paperwhite represents quite an upgrade from the standard Kindle line of e-reader devices. Its standout feature is its backlit screen. The Kindle's e-ink display has become very popular since it was introduced and remains so, but, up until now, it did have its limitations. The Paperwhite offers a way for you to enjoy your favorite Kindle books on a screen that requires no book light when you're reading in a dimly lit— or even completely dark—room. The backlight feature is also useful in lit rooms and outdoors, where it does great job of increasing the contrast of the pages you're reading.

The Kindle Paperwhite is competitively priced and has the kinds of features that e-reader users will very much appreciate, and plenty more. The first thing you're likely to notice when you fire up your Kindle Paperwhite is the clarity of the display, which features 62% more pixels than the older generation of Kindle e-readers. The improvements to the Kindle Paperwhite go far beyond this, however, and you're likely to be very pleased when you start reading your favorite books and magazines on this compact, advanced e-reader.

Price Points and Options

The Kindle Paperwhite offers you quite a few choices in terms of variations, with versions with no advertising costing slightly more than the simpler versions. There are two major things that separate price points on these devices between the 4 options: the advertising and optional 3G connectivity.

The basic specs that apply to all models of the Kindle Paperwhite include the following. The variations are listed below:

- Built-in LED illumination

- 6 font styles

- 8 font sizes

- Built in Wi-Fi

- Up to 8 weeks of battery life @ 10% illumination and 30 minutes per day reading

- 63% more pixels than other Kindle models

- 25% improved contrast than other Kindle models

- Prime Kindle Owner's Lending Library access with Prime subscription

- 2GB of internal storage

- Screen size 6"

- Total size 6.7" x 4.6"x .36"

- Weight 7.5 ounces

The Kindle Paperwhite with Special Offers

The Kindle Paperwhite with special offers included—which means that the device will serve you advertisements based on what you're reading—costs $119. This device has Wi-Fi connectivity built into it, but no mobile Internet connectivity capabilities. For some people, the advertisements may be distractions—they appear on your home screen—but for others they may be handy, as they tend to be targeted toward your reading habits and may just give you some great recommendations.

The Kindle Paperwhite Without Special Offers

For $139, you can get an advertisement-free version of the basic Kindle Paperwhite. This version has the same features as the Kindle Paperwhite with advertisements, but doesn't have the offers that some people might find distracting.

The Kindle Paperwhite 3G with Special Offers

For $179, you can get a version of the Kindle Paperwhite with free 3G wireless connectivity built into it. The "free" part of that comes with no catch. You won't have to select a carrier, pay a monthly fee for your 3G or deal with any third parties. This version of the Kindle Paperwhite also comes with Wi-Fi connectivity built into it, so you don't' have to use the 3G network full time. This version does include advertisements.

The Kindle Paperwhite 3G Without Special Offers

This would be the deluxe version of the Kindle Paperwhite. It has all of the options as far as features go, including the 3G connectivity, with no advertising at all. This version is the most expensive, costing $199.

Any one of the Kindle Paperwhite options features the same non-glare, high-resolution screen and the backlight that defines this device as something new in the e-reader world.

About the Ads

The advertisements, or "special offers", as Amazon calls them, appear on your home screen, on the bottom, and on the
10

screensaver. The ads will not appear when you're reading and don't distract from that experience. There are pros and cons to the advertisements that you may want to consider.

Pros:

- The ads are targeted and may let you know when new books by your favorite authors are out.

- Shopping on the device is very easy, more so with the advertisements.

- The advertisements don't interfere with actual reading.

Cons:

- Some people find the ads a nuisance and want total control of the device.

- The screensaver ads may annoy some users.

- The ads do take up screen space.

Remember that you can unsubscribe from special offers from the Manage Your Kindle page under Your Account if you buy one of the less expensive models and change your mind about the ads.

What Makes the Paperwhite Different?

The Kindle Paperwhite differs from previous versions of the popular Amazon e-reader device in more ways than the lighted screen. Setting it up, however, is largely the same as is setting up any other Amazon Kindle e-reader or Kindle Fire. The first thing you need to do is register the device, which hooks it up to your cloud storage and to your Amazon account in general.

When you fire up the device for the first time, you will be presented with the option to register your device, connect to a Wi-Fi network and given some tutorial screens to help you to understand how to use the device.

First, you have to select your language. After you select your language, you will have to connect to a Wi-Fi network to register your device. This is extremely easy to do. The screens will guide you through the process so all you have to do is select your Wi-Fi network, enter your Wi-Fi password and you'll be online. There are probably numbers in your password. To access the numerical keys on your keyboard, tap the key labeled "123!?" and you'll get the keyboard with the numbers on it. Select "connect" and you will be connected to the Wi-Fi network. The Kindle Paperwhite will remember your networks and connect to them automatically as they become available.

Registering

Registering your device is very easy. If you have an Amazon account already, simply select the option to use an existing Amazon account, enter your username and password and the process is automatic. If you need to create a new account, you will need to select that option, enter a payment method for purchases made on your Kindle and you'll be ready to go. Once you have your device registered, it's connected to your Amazon account and you can make purchases and take advantage of all the other features that the site offers.

Charging the Battery

The battery life on the Kindle Paperwhite, to put it mildly, is phenomenal. For an average user, the Kindle Paperwhite should be able to give approximately 8 weeks of battery life for one charge, according to Amazon. Keep in mind that this includes using the backlight feature. What this means is that you're going to spend very little time actually charging this device. Charging the device is very simple. You may purchase a wall charger adapter or hook it up to a USB port with the mini USB cable included with the Kindle Paperwhite. The LED near the power switch will glow amber when the device is charging and switch to green when it is fully charged.

Your Kindle Paperwhite will likely not arrive fully charged. It is a good idea to charge the battery fully once you receive it.

It should take approximately 4 hours to charge the device from 0% to 100% of battery capacity using a USB port. Using an accessory charger may reduce this charge time considerably, and some options are listed in the last chapter of the book.

Hooking the Device to Your Computer

Hooking your Kindle Paperwhite up to your computer is very easy. All you have to do is plug the mini USB cable into the port on the device and plug the USB end of the cable into your computer. You shouldn't have any trouble at all with your computer recognizing the device and it will show up as another drive on your computer. Hooking your Kindle up to your computer is one of the easiest ways to charge it and, of course, you'll want to do this if you want to transfer e-books from your computer onto your device.

The Kindle Paperwhite is amazingly simple for all of its powerful features. After you have the battery charged, the device registered and you're hooked up to a Wi-Fi network, you're ready to go.

The Amazon Cloud

The Amazon Cloud storage service, part of AWS (Amazon Web Services), provides a backup storage feature for your Kindle Paperwhite. You don't have to do anything technical to take advantage of it. In fact, it's already working on your Paperwhite right now.

What it Does

Any content that you buy from Amazon is automatically backed up in the cloud. If you're not familiar with the term "cloud" as it applies to digital storage, it's essentially a form of storage that's available over any Internet connection. As the owner of a Paperwhite, it means is that you get to back up your content on a vast network of storage servers provided by Amazon. Amazon offers other cloud-based services, as well, such as streaming music from the cloud, but the Kindle Paperwhite is exclusively a reading device, so those services do not apply to the Paperwhite specifically. Where the Paperwhite is concerned, it just backs up all of your books.

Whenever you buy an eBook from Amazon, it's automatically added to your cloud drive. You download it to your device by going to the Cloud storage section on your homepage and tapping its icon to download it. You can remove materials from your Paperwhite by pressing and holding their icon on the Device section of your home screen and selecting "Remove from Device" from the menu that pops up.

Remember that you have 2GB of storage on your Kindle Paperwhite, so there's really little chance that space is going to be an issue at any point.

Amazon has extensive cloud-based services, which you may want to explore for their own benefits. Where your Kindle Paperwhite is concerned, however, you're already given the benefit of having your books backed up for you.

Important Note

If you do not have 3G and there are no Wi-Fi networks available, you won't be able to access content that you have stored in the cloud. If you're going on a long trip or you have another reason that you want to keep a good selection of books handy, verify that they're stored on your device before you leave. Anything in the cloud requires that you have a live Internet connection to access it. If a file is listed on your Device page on your Home screen, it's stored locally and you can access it without an Internet connection.

Basics

The first time you hook up to a Wi-Fi network, it will be as part of the setup process, which means that the Kindle will guide you through it. You may need to hook up to a different Wi-Fi network when you're out and about. Again, the Kindle Paperwhite makes this very easy.

Wi-Fi Networks

Tap the Menu icon ☰ , which you will find located on the upper right-hand side of your home screen. Select "Settings" and then select "Wi-Fi Networks". You'll get a list of the wireless networks in range. If you don't see the network you are looking for, select "Rescan" and see if it shows up. Select the network, enter the password and you will be hooked up to the Wi-Fi. Remember, the Kindle will remember this network so, if you are in range of it again, the Kindle will automatically connect. This is a great feature if you happen to use your device in a coffee shop or another location with a free wireless hotspot.

3G Connectivity

If you have the 3G model, your Kindle will automatically hook up to 3G wireless networks when you're not hooked up to a

Wi-Fi network. This device works in over 100 nations, so you have 3G connectivity just about anywhere in the world you happen to travel. There are some limitations on the 3G connectivity, however. The principal one is that, if you choose to use the experimental browser feature on the Kindle, you can only access Amazon.com and Wikipedia if you are using the 3G connection.

If you happen to be on an airplane, you'll be required to turn off any wireless devices. You can do this from the settings menu and select "Airplane Mode". This allows you to keep reading on your Kindle while you are in the air, but to do so without violating the requirement that any wireless devices be turned off.

When you are hooked up to a 3G network, you will see "3G", "EDGE" or "GPRS" displayed in the upper right-hand corner of the device. If you're hooked up to a Wi-Fi connection, you will see "Wi-Fi" with a single indicator displayed in the upper right-hand corner of the device. The main thing to remember about 3G connectivity if you happen to have a Kindle Paperwhite that's equipped with it is that you really don't have to do anything to take advantage of it.

The Keyboard

The Kindle Paperwhite comes with an on-screen keyboard that will pop up whenever you put the cursor in a field where you can enter text or when you are executing a search. It is, for the most part, a thought-free process to utilize this. There are three different keyboards available to you on the Kindle Paperwhite. The first keyboard that pops up will give you all the letters of the alphabet, with the option to make capitals. Select the key labeled "123!?" to access the numerical keys and additional punctuation keys. On that second keyboard, select the key labeled "#~=" to be taken to a third keyboard that gives you the option to access less commonly used symbols, currency symbols and other keys. Select "ABC" from that screen and you'll be brought back to the original keyboard. As far as the keyboard on the Kindle Paperwhite goes, that's really all there is to it.

Navigating Books

Tap Zones

Navigating books on the Kindle Paperwhite is extremely easy. This will be covered in greater detail in the next chapter, but there are two different tap regions on the touchscreen. On the top of the touchscreen, you can tap your finger and access the main menu. You can also advance pages by simply tapping on the left-hand portion of the screen, which would've been illustrated to you in the setup tutorial.

Landscape/Portrait

The Kindle Paperwhite gives to the option to read in landscape or portrait mode. Portrait is the default orientation. To switch to landscape mode, tap your finger in the upper portion of the screen, select the Menu key and select Landscape Mode from the list of options you're presented with.

The Backlight

The backlight is really what separates the Kindle Paperwhite for most of the other e-reader models out there on the market. To access the control for the backlight, start by tapping in the upper portion of the screen to bring up the main menu. You'll find a small light bulb icon on the top of the screen. By tapping this icon, you bring up an intensity slider that allows you to select an appropriate illumination level for the conditions you're reading it. If you are in a well-lit room, you'll find that turning the backlight off completely gives you the same sort of clear and easy-to-read text that you would expect from any Kindle e-reader. To add more light, simply move the slider up.

One of the great things about the backlight feature on this particular e-reader is that it doesn't actually blast light right into your face. The light is directed so that it illuminates the page on the book, which gives you a great deal of clarity without lighting up an entire room when you turn on the light. Not only is it more convenient than using a standard book light, it's also a lot more pleasant for the people around you, who may be distracted by the book light.

The Kindle Paperwhite is really made for reading, so let's look at how that's done on this device right now.

Reading on the Kindle Paperwhite

When you first set up your Kindle Paperwhite, you'll be taken through a series of screens that show you where the tap zones on the touchscreen are located. To access the main menu, simply tap the top section of the screen. The main menu will also give you options to "Go To" a particular place in your book, and by selecting the magnifying glass icon, you can search your book for words or phrases.

On the very right of the main menu, just below the home screen icon, you'll find "Aa". One of the standout features of the Kindle Paperwhite is the flexibility it offers you in terms of fonts. You can choose from six different fonts, or use the publisher font. You can also change the margins on the display and change the line spacing. Of course, you can also change the font size, which makes it a lot easier for some people to read.

The Kindle Paperwhite makes it easy to get books from Amazon, add books from your computer and offers you the option to store your books in the cloud or on the device itself. Let's start by learning how to get books.

Getting Books

Any books you've already purchased for a Kindle device will be available to you through your Amazon account. To access these books, go to the home screen, and look on the upper left-hand portion of the screen. You will see "Cloud | Device" listed among the options. This functions as a toggle switch. If the word "Cloud" is highlighted, you're looking at the content you have stored on the Amazon cloud. If the word "Device" is highlighted, you're looking at books that are stored locally on your device.

To download anything from your cloud account, all you have to do is tap on it and it will be delivered over 3G or Wi-Fi, depending upon the network that you're hooked up to. To remove the book from your device that you downloaded from the cloud, simply press and hold the icon on the home screen for that book and a menu will pop up, giving you the option to remove it from the device. There is 2G of internal storage on the device, so you likely do not have much to worry about as far as running out of space is concerned, unless you're storing very large documents.

If you want to go shopping at Amazon, it's no more difficult than selecting the shopping cart icon on the top of the screen. You can use the "Search" field to look for a specific book or you can browse through books using the categories presented to you.

The Kindle Paperwhite comes with two gigabytes of onboard storage, which is enough to hold roughly 1,000 books. Combined with Amazon cloud storage, you should never run out of room for your library.

The Kindle Owner's Lending Library

The Kindle Owner's Lending Library is available for Amazon Prime members. It's amazing. There are nearly 150,000 books available to members. You can check them out, read them and never have to worry about a return date. These books include current and former best sellers, some of the most popular series in the world and more.

To access this resource, go to the Kindle Store on your device and tap on the "Kindle Owner's Lending Library entry under "All Categories". When a book can be borrowed, it has "Prime" listed next to its entry. When you open up the book description, simply click "Borrow for Free" and start reading!

The Public Library

You can check out books from your local library and read them on your Kindle Paperwhite, depending upon whether or not your library is participating in this feature. There are in excess of 11,000 libraries that are participating, so there's a good chance that this feature is, indeed, available to you!

Your library's policies will dictate checkout times. You'll have to use a system called Overdrive to use this feature, which you download to your computer according to the instructions from your library.

There is kind of an unusual aspect to this feature. Some publishers will not allow their books to be delivered over Wi-Fi or wireless connections. In such cases, you'll have to download the book to your desktop computer and transfer it over to your Kindle using a mini USB cable.

If you can do this wirelessly, here are the instructions:

- Go to your library's page and select a book available in Kindle format to check out.

- Use your library card to check out the book.

- Go to your Amazon account page and choose to have the book delivered to your Kindle.

- If you cannot, download it to your computer and then follow the instructions to deliver it to your device over a mini USB. There is also an option to do this on the Amazon account page, "Download & Transfer via USB".

TIP: The great thing about this feature is that you'll never get late fees. When the checkout period has expired, the book is automatically removed from your device.

Public Domain Books

There are thousands of books in the public domain and Amazon has a vast selection of them. These are books that have fallen out of copyright and that you can get for free, without ever crossing that ugly line into Internet piracy.

If you're looking for any of the classics, be sure you check for versions that come at no cost. Amazon has a surprising number of them and, after all, if you want a copy of Frankenstein, there's no sense paying for it if you don't have to.

Samples

When you're shopping for books, you'll run across some that offer you a free sample. This is one of the best ways to explore new genres, authors or books. Select to download the sample and you won't be billed a thing and can take a look at the first portion of a book to get an idea of whether or not is something you'd like to read!

Other Document Formats

Your Kindle Paperwhite supports documents in the following formats:

- BMP (requires conversion)

- DOC

- DOCX

- GIF

- HTML

- JPEG

- Kindle (AZW)

- Kindle Format 8 (AZW3)

- PDF

- PNG

- PRC natively

- TXT

- unsecured MOBI

Remember that not all of these document formats will support all of the features that the Kindle Paperwhite offers. For example, not every e-book you purchase will support the X-ray feature, which is discussed in a later chapter.

Panel View

Panel view provides you with an easy way to read comics and Manga on your Kindle Paperwhite. In order for you to use this feature, however, you have to purchase books that are designed for Kindle Panel View. You'll find them in the Amazon store and they're denoted as supporting this feature.

To use panel view, open up your comic or Manga book. You'll be presented with the full-page view. To activate Panel View, simply double tap on the panel you want to see. This will enlarge the panel so that it's easy to read. You can progress through the panels on the page, and to the next page, by tapping on the screen.

Remember that this won't work with comics that don't have the feature included, but many of the most popular comic books, graphic novels and Manga books out there are already available with the feature built into them.

Zooming

The zooming feature on e-books makes them accessible for anyone. If you have trouble reading small print or if you want to reduce the amount of time you spend paging through your book, you can make the text larger or smaller with a few taps.

There are two ways to do this. The easiest way is to simply tap on the top of the screen and select the "Aa" button, which will give you an option to increase the font size; simply select the next largest font size, or the next smallest one, according to your preference.

You can also use the pinching and spreading motions with your fingers on the touch screen to access the font size menu without pulling up the full menu of font options or the main menu. Spread or pinch your fingers on the touchscreen and a selection of font sizes will pop up. Unlike some touch screen devices, however, the Kindle Paperwhite won't pull or pinch the font size larger or smaller by simply following your finger motions.

Dictionaries

Go to your Cloud storage and page through the entries until you find one labeled "Dictionaries". Just as the name says, there's a selection of dictionaries in this folder that provide you with several different language options. Select the dictionary you want and it will be available when you want to look up a word.

To access the dictionary while you're reading, tap and hold the word that you want information on for a second. When you lift your finger, the definition will appear. To set your default dictionary, download the one you want from the cloud, go to the Menu button, select "Device Options" and then select "Language and Dictionaries".

TIP: One of the great things about the Kindle Paperwhite is that you can set different default dictionaries for different languages. If you speak more than one language, or are studying a different language, this is a great tool!

Notes

Notes are great for anyone who is serious about their books. If you want to write down something important to a plot, trace a narrative or plot line or just add notes to a textbook you're using for a class, this feature is excellent.

- Tap on a word where you want to add the note and release it after about a second

- In the dialog the pops up, select "More"

- Select "Add Note"

- Fill in your note and save it

After you do this, a number will appear next to the word. Tap on that word and you'll get access to your note and options to edit it. To delete the note, click "More" and choose the option to delete the note.

Searching and Highlighting

Again, these are great features for students and for people who take their literature seriously.

To search for a term of phrase, tap on the top of the screen to bring up the menu. Select the magnifying glass icon and enter the terms you're interested in and enter, just as you would on any other search field. A list that shows the occurrences of the term you're interested in from the book will pop up with the term or phrase highlighted. Tap on the location to go to that instance of the term or terms you're searching for.

To highlight text, tap and hold your finger on the word or tap, hold and drag your finger across a passage. When you lift up your finger, you'll get the option to make a highlight. Do delete the highlight, simply repeat the process and select "Delete" from the menu that pops up when you lift your finger.

X-Ray

X-ray is an advanced search feature that can give you some interesting information about anything you happen to be reading, provided the feature is enabled for that book. Not all titles will have this feature. If the title you're reading does, however, it can give you some interesting information.

Tap on the top of the screen to bring up the menu. Along the bottom row of options, you'll see "X-Ray". If it's grayed out, it means that X-ray is not enabled for the title that you're reading. If it is, tap on it.

X-ray allows you to get information on characters, to go to Wikipedia articles about the book and to get in-depth information on what you're reading, as well. This is a great feature for anyone who wants to get a more in-depth look at what they're reading and who wants to engage in some analysis of their favorite books.

Bookmarks

Your Kindle Paperwhite will automatically remember where you left off in a chapter. Whispersync will also make sure that, if you access a book on your cloud account from any other device, your bookmarks will carry over. Making a bookmark is easy.

Tap on the top of the screen

Select the Menu button

Select "Add Bookmark"

Viewing Notes, Bookmarks and Highlights

- Tap on the top of the screen

- Select the menu key

- Select View Notes and Marks

To go to any of the entries that pop up, simply tap them.

Popular Highlights

When you're paging through some books, you might find some passages labeled as "Popular Highlight". These represent sections of the book that were highlighted by many different people. If you select to view notes, bookmarks and highlights as described above, you might see some of these. They provide a great way to get more insight about a book and what parts of it tend to be the most meaningful to readers.

Public Notes

These are the note equivalents of popular highlights. These are notes that are added to a book and made public by the person who added it. You have to turn this feature on for it to work, so don't worry about other people reading what you added to a book. You can turn this feature on and off by going to the Your Books page, located at https://kindle.amazon.com/your_reading.

Some of the people who add notes to books include professors, literary critics and others who have a great deal of knowledge. If you're reading something for serious study—or even just for fun—be sure to check if there are any public notes added. Remember, however, that they may contain spoilers, so you might want to do this after you're done with a book if you want to make sure that the suspense isn't ruined.

The Kindle Paperwhite has some exciting advanced features. The next chapter will give you all the pertinent info.

Advanced Features

The Kindle Paperwhite is more than meets the eye. While it's a great e-reader, it also has some advanced features built into that make it a tool for social networking and even web browsing. Here are some of the great things that you can do with your Kindle Paperwhite, some of which can make reading a downright social activity!

Social Networking

You'll be prompted to set up your social networks when you first set up the device, but you may not have chosen to do so right away. If you want to do so afterward, it's very easy.

- Go to the Settings Menu from the home screen

- Select "Settings"

- Select "Reading Options"

- Select "Social Networks"

- Select to connect your Twitter or Facebook account

- Select a Pen Name

The social networking features allow you to share excerpts from the books you're reading right on your feed or your wall. When you share these messages, they will also be linked to the Kindle page at Kindle.Amazon.com under your pen name.

This is a great way for you to keep a dialogue going about books with your avid reader friends and to share parts of books you find particularly important or meaningful.

Syncing Books

The Kindle Paperwhite makes this very easy to do. When you purchase something from Amazon, it's automatically added to your cloud storage and you can download it to your device by tapping on it.

If you're using the 3G connection and want to sync your device, go to the home screen, select Menu and select Synch and Check for Items. If you have pending items, they'll be downloaded after you do this. If something isn't downloading, be sure you have it pending. Go to the Mange your Kindle page on Amazon and look under "Your Pending Deliveries". This will let you know whether the content is actually in the queue.

As a last resort, just try rebooting your Kindle and see if that solves the issue.

Syncing is much faster on Wi-Fi and downloading large content on your device over 3G may take more time that you expected. A progress bar on the upper left-hand side of the screen will let you know if something is downloading or not.

When you do access books across devices, they will be synced. For example, if you leave off on Chapter 5 of a book on your Kindle Paperwhite and want to read it on your smartphone later in the day, sync the device and it will come up exactly where you left off.

Experimental Browser

The experimental browser on the Paperwhite is, not too surprisingly, very experimental. It's not going to display webpages with the beautiful results that you'd get from a Kindle Fire or Kindle Fire HD, but it's good in a pinch. If you're on your 3G connection, the browser will only allow you to visit the Amazon homepage or Wikipedia.

That said, the experimental browser is handy. You can check email on Gmail accounts with it, for example, and on other services, as well. The display will be black and white, of course, but you do get the great readability of the high-contrast, high-resolution screen that characterizes the Kindle Paperwhite. Be aware that loading is sometimes a bit slow and that images will not display as beautifully as you'd likely prefer. Scrolling isn't as smooth as it is on a true tablet computer, but this browser is really an enhancement in that you can do some research beyond what X-ray and the other features on the Kindle Paperwhite offer.

Accessories and Enhancements

The Kindle Paperwhite is remarkably compact and light. It's also an electronic device, of course, which means that it merits some protection and that there are some accessories that you'll likely want to get to go along with your Paperwhite.

There are plenty of different options for accessories for this device, some of which you may or may not have a need for. The most popular ones are listed here for you to consider.

Covers

Covers give you the closest experience to reading a book that you're going to get using an e-reader. They secure your e-reader on one side of the cover and the other folds over the top, protecting the screen while you're transporting it. The other nice feature about covers is that they make the very thin Paperwhite thicker, which makes it easier to hold onto the device when you're reading.

There are some covers out there that are portfolio designs. These have extra pockets and other features that may make them useful for people who need to carry accessories along with their Kindle. Remember, however, to be wary of using interior pockets, as these may fold over the screen when you close the device. If you do use such a cover, be sure you don't put anything that will damage the screen in the pocket opposite your Kindle Paperwhite!

TIP: The Kindle Paperwhite may well fit into a case for another e-reader you already own. Before you go buy another one, check to make sure!

You can purchase cases from Amazon or from third party sellers. You can even purchase handmade, customized ones from sites such as Etsy. Be sure to explore your options in this regard, as it's a great way to personalize your Kindle Paperwhite and because it really can make the reading experience quite a bit different.

Sleeves

Sleeves are protective cases for your Paperwhite that don't fold out like a book., They come in a wide variety of designs and offer you a safe place to store your Kindle Paperwhite, though you'll be holding the device in your hand while you're reading if you go this route.

If you're going to use a sleeve, be sure you pick one that fits your Kindle Paperwhite very well, as a loose case will allow it to move around and may cause scratches or other damage.

A sleeve is sometimes a great way to give your Kindle Paperwhite some extra protection when you're going somewhere that exposure to the elements is a hazard. Even if you have a cover, you may want to consider putting your Paperwhite into a case if you're dropping it into a backpack or somewhere else that it might be damaged by other objects.

Chargers

There's quite a bit of flexibility where chargers are concerned. You can buy devices that allow you to plug the mini USB cord into a wall socket via a converter. You can also buy devices that are standalone chargers, which allow you to plug in and charge your Kindle Paperwhite without having to use a mini USB cable.

Remember to be careful with these choices. Some chargers may end up causing damage to your Kindle because they're not compatible in terms of voltage or current. The safest way to get the right charger for your device is to go to Amazon and look at what they have available.

Amazon has some accelerated chargers available for Kindle devices. These allow you to charge your Kindle much more quickly than you'd be able to using a USB, which is a handy feature, indeed!

Travelling

If you're travelling outside of the US, be sure you look into power converters to make sure you'll be able to charge your device off of a wall socket. Alternately, you can stick to the mini USB and charge off a computer.

Screen Protectors

The first time you fired up your Kindle Paperwhite, you were probably taken aback by how beautiful the screen is. This is, in part, because it is designed to have a no-glare surface. You'll also notice that the screen has a textured feel to it. Hold it in the light and you'll immediately notice that you don't leave the same trail of fingerprints and palm prints that you leave on most tablet computers. Do you need a screen protector for this device? It's really a matter of preference.

The Kindle Paperwhite has a very durable screen. Unless you do something genuinely irresponsible with it, the screen will likely hold up for the lifetime of the device. Additionally, it's not a cell phone, which means that you're not likely to toss it in your pocket or purse with your keys, you're not going to be holding it up to your face, throwing it on the car seat next to you and so forth. Some e-reader users skip the screen protector and just use a case for protection.

The alternate view is that, since you paid for the device, you might as well do everything short of wrapping it in bubble wrap to keep it safe. A screen protector can protect your device against some common hazards. For instance, if you are a student and toss the Paperwhite in your backpack, the screen protector may end up saving your device from getting scratched by keys, pens and other implements that might be floating around in your backpack. A screen protector also reduces glare but, on the Paperwhite, glare is a non-issues.

If you're going to apply a screen protector, the following process will keep you from getting frustrated doing it.

- Wipe down the screen with a microfiber cloth until it's as clean as you can get it. Pay attention to the edges.

- Use canned air to blast off any remaining dust.

- Apply the screen protector slowly, starting at one end of the screen and working your way across. If there are bubbles under the screen protector that keep it from adhering, you probably have dust on the adhesive side of the protector.

- Remove the dust by using a piece of masking tape and pulling the dust off of the adhesive side of the screen protector with the adhesive side of the masking tape.

Place them adhesive side to adhesive side and peel away the masking tape, and the dust will come with it.

- Make another attempt at applying the screen protector.

- Do this until the screen protector is completely flat, there are no bubbles and the screen is easy to read.

If you have trouble doing this, don't feel like it's because you're technically inept. There are forum posts and even YouTube videos dedicated to teaching people how to do this!

Skins

Skins are somewhat like the cases that people put on cell phone. They're not covers or cases, as they don't have any folding part. They slide over the device itself and allow you a means of personalizing it and offering it a bit more protection against damage. If a cover is too bulky for you or if you just want to personalize your device a bit, you can use one of these.

Unlike covers, skins have to fit precisely. Be sure that you choose a cover that specifically says that it fits the Paperwhite, as not all of them will and you'll end up having to buy a new cover if you choose the wrong size!

Extended Warranties

These really aren't accessories, but they're available in the same section of the Amazon site as other accessories for the Kindle Paperwhite. The warranty options vary, but there are two variations available at present.

The 2-Year Protection Plan for Kindle Paperwhite

This is available for US Paperwhite owners only. The package is only available for Paperwhite that were purchased 30 days or less before you purchased the warranty. The coverage includes protection against accidental damage for 2 years. This damage includes liquids, cracked screens, drops and more. The plan gives more detailed information on what's included.

If your battery goes bad within the two-year coverage period, you can replace it, but you can only use this option once.

The coverage varies by year. For the first year, the device will be covered for electronic and mechanical failures by the manufacturer, with the protection plan taking over during the second year. Accidental damage is covered for both years by this protection plan. You can transfer this coverage if you purchase the device for someone else and there are no deductibles or shipping fees if you have to use the warranty coverage terms.

Probably the most important feature about this warranty is that it stays with the device, which makes it a good way to insure a Paperwhite given as a gift.

This plan costs $29.99.

The 2-Year Protection Plan for Kindle Paperwhite 3-G

If you have the 3G variation of the Kindle Paperwhite, you'll need to purchase this plan. It covers the same things that the other plan covers, but also covers the additional features on the 3G. Make sure you get the right plan.

This coverage plan costs $39.99.

Like the standard Paperwhite warranty, this one transfers with the device. Electrical and mechanical failures are covered by this warranty in year 2, but are covered by the manufacturer warranty in year 1.

Amazon Prime

You'll get a free trial of Amazon Prime with your Kindle Purchase. This allows you to get a look at the Kindle Owner's

Lending Library, in addition to all the other benefits—free 2-day shipping on many items, free movies, etc.—that go along with this package. If you're an avid reader, this membership may pay for itself very quickly. It's definitely something to consider for any Kindle Paperwhite owner!

Enjoy!

There is more to explore on the Kindle Paperwhite, and you'll be well prepared to do so having gone through what was described in this book. Be sure to check out the other features that your Kindle Paperwhite offers.

E-readers have revolutionized the way that people enjoy literature, whether they're reading the classics, a celebrity gossip magazine or a pulp fiction magazine. The Kindle Paperwhite has taken this a step farther, simply by making the device easier to read in varied light conditions and by offering incredible clarity and resolution. Cared for properly, this device will give you many hours of enjoyment. Because it is connected to the cloud, your library will endure, even if you switch devices, so enjoy your purchase and all that it offers you!

www.ingramcontent.com/pod-product-compliance
Lightning Source LLC
Chambersburg PA
CBHW071033050326
40689CB00014B/3638